Grace Cohen is a performance poet, perpetual student, and chronic over-sharer. Originally from Bristol, she has performed in festivals, bars, and bedrooms around the United Kingdom, winning the annual WOMAD festival slam, and representing Bristol in the Hammer and Tongue Slam national final at The Royal Albert Hall. She is currently working towards her MA in English Literature at Goldsmiths College, London.

Calling This Body Home

Grace Cohen

Burning Eye

Calling This Body Home

For Georgie and Eddie

and for Ethan

CONTENTS

CALLING THIS BODY HOME

oh loved one, the sky is slowly mushrooming into orange

how you cluck and fuss
over the city

wipe dirt from its cheek
with your thumb

by winter my thoughts
had started to curl at the edges

I am still pushing creases
from my brow like a sheet

overhead, the birds talk politics
note you're still here

the river parades itself in front of us
like a toddler in a new dress

surely the water must ache by now
it is July and you're still here

and I have begun calling
this body home again

oh loved one, you looked
like you were sat on nervousness

stood so still, like the last child
at the school gate

COME WITH ME

for Rachel

come with me
it would be too easy
for you to spend
another day in bed
instead we'll roam these streets

let your feet beat back the pavement into submission
let us chase the howling hounds
of wind sent from the peaks
these streets, they're kissed
with the frost of a morning
you don't yet believe in
come worship it with me

let us navigate the curves
of the derelict monster
who squats over Broomhill
with bones packed full
of days we can but wonder at
let's sit between its brows
and watch the sun set
over this volcanoed city
until the streetlamps peek
through the ash like embers

and remember those alien days

when you couldn't get out of bed
when shallow breaths
barely disturbed dust motes
waiting for a breeze
when gathering dust
covered a dry harbour of cotton
wrapped around a glass copy of you

you say your flesh is not your own
that it was gifted to you
by your mother
to be guarded
waiting for a child
now half-hidden in a stranger

but you are the fruit
of a million labours
prehistoric calls echo in your veins
I can see the flames of those first fires
redden your cheeks
when I tell you this

know you were not born to wait

in summer gold fields ripple
in bent bodies of grass
for you, for you, for you
for you can ignite a light
to end an empire
your thoughts are a blaze
no man can touch
like moths to them we turn
your bones they are steel
and your eyes
they burn

see, that smile could eclipse
a distant sun
and could spark this city
into something almighty
if only you could see
not kindling waiting for a flame
you and me
we are all made of fire

A VANISHING ACT IN FOUR PARTS

Monday is a day dedicated to trying very hard
trying is invariably tried at work
in the bath, and in bed
food is consumed etc. etc.

on Tuesday I spend the day
thinking about snow
how it lounges around so decadently
trips up strangers
and doesn't even feel guilt

I start finding splinters
in the soles of my feet
on Wednesday night
first flecks of glass
picked from scabs, healing
half-heartedly
then a thumb-sized shard
slides out, miraculously clean
finally, with a magician's flourish
I pull a sliver of metal
from the dead
centre of my right heel
I bow, and the audience cheer
from my bedside table
as I put myself under

the rest of the week, I am not seen
and my sadness is clutter
singing out from the drawer

THERE ARE SEVEN DOG SHITS ON MY ROAD

and seven dogs who planned this, waiting until I was not quite
    settled
in my new room, in my new city
where I can go days
without seeing grass
– seven dog owners who
when I say *I love your dog*
look at me as though I have said
I want to make love to your dog

seven mornings to wake up heavy
and seven people on the tube
giving me side-eye
but there are only seven more commutes until you are here
and softly arguing with you
feels as comforting as standing barefoot
on slices of cheap white bread

London is as lovely as rubble
broken up into pieces
small enough to drink
but when you are here
you dredge the lake
that has been growing in me

your hand feels like getting
into a freshly made bed
and as we walk
the cracks in the street
heal under our step

ON HIBERNATION

I'm obsessed with teeth
I have forty-eight
shall I tell you their names?
their siblings, should you see
their family tree
(of course you want to know
none of this)
shall I show you what they can do?

I have no fillings
look me in the mouth
see behind my tonsils
the cavernous echo
small prehistoric birds building nests
or homes
in the cilia
closer still
       the crack of shell, hinting
       at a beak
see the precious metal
the minable ore
my lungs are full of oil

now magpies no longer follow me
I have folded in all summer
allowed no fresh air
a detox of sight
– when winter arrives
I will put my eyes back in
while my love
sings to no one
in the kitchen

TWO LADYBIRDS

one wasp, one dragonfly
a spider, a weevil
and several small mites I don't know
wait with me
while you are at work
Cambridge is odd when alone
but if I could write a poem anywhere
it would be here, surely

if I could write a poem
anywhere, it would touch on
the confusion that arises
purely from the texture of your lips

it would touch on how the bed
feels like an enormous boat
adrift in a very small room
on which we sleep soundly as drunks
save for the tick of your tin heart
and my trigger finger's itch
to harpoon a passing star

THANK YOU

I told you you didn't need to stay
my heart running laps
in my chest, the flutter
of a trapped bird wing
you said nothing
but when morning came
bringing with it reality
I woke in the life raft
of your limbs

this is not a love poem
I cannot write them for you anymore

this is a thank-you
for how you allowed me
to haunt your body for weeks
held me as my tears
rusted holes in my skin
for how you bowed your back
to carry my skeleton
and never once told me
that I was too heavy
or that it will all be okay

my mother told me
the world is divided
into those that know death
and those that don't
my life is divided into before and after
and you were my bridge
heard the howl of the earth
splitting open and you lay down
across it, this is a thank you

you hardly knew me
yet you showed me how
to hold a soul in the cradle of ribcage

to turn your arms into hammock nets
and rock them as they fade

I taught you
that grief is a long-range missile
firing down wires to find
its target at the end of a telephone
a silent explosion
leaving only that moan
they make in the movies
that I never understood
until it poured over my tongue
and choked me

I was shaking like an addict
like a branch in a hurricane
I was crying
before she even said the words

that room is one of my worst
blank cell, compressing inch
by inch, hands stumbling
over fingertips, Morse code
I can't believe it

the globe became a map
of misinformation
with the media making
the seedier story
turning boy into headline
– line into bullet
each round that hit, I'd whisper
they didn't know shit about him

whilst your hands
stroked the thunderstorm in my voice
as it turned into rain again

thank you for understanding
that it could not be fixed

you just curled around me
like an ampersand
and when we woke
the mourning was so crisp
you started to fold it
into origami boats

THIS DISPOSABLE CAMERA

contains the last picture I took of you
before you died, and I know
this small box shouldn't tug
at the piece of string
I've tied round my finger
but for me, you are as much beneath
that green lawn with your name on top as you are in Tesco
picking up bread right now

it keeps catching my eye, saying
there's a poem in that
or a picture of you
or really it contains my fear
– a few blank frames
and the knowledge
that you are as much in there
as you are anywhere

SALTFORD

the river soothed itself
under the bridge
while we became machines
trading legs for wheels
and spinning

the sun swallowed into a violet
caught itself between banks brimming
with what was not yet loss
as we swam

prayers paused
surveyed themselves
while others, caught by aeroplanes
cut the sky
into kitchen knives

wish you were here

MARE TRANQUILLITATIS

what a weight
a leaden press of
fresh sunflowers

stone saints cling
to this place and
that cloud of incense
is threatening rain

she is the thunderstorm break
          in the pressure
the terrible lighting
lightening of a load
when she arrives, we
all busy ourselves
with the business
of saying goodbye

now pressed under train light
my head fractures to
each punch
of the tracks
and stinging my ears
is the insect buzz of
second-hand headphones

I crave the freedom
of a feather-light darkness
shared with none
give me an expanse of sheets
that shed my weight
into sleep
and forgive my skin
give me the soft melting
of an empty room

give me a sea of silence
          to drown my thoughts in

GIRL

this girl is a blank canvas
soon to be painted
with heritage
until then, she breathes free
from the weight that is woman
there is a reason that lipstick
comes in bullets
this girl kisses every single one
feels the fire between her thighs
and cries water like steam

this girl is a garden
her soil grew his hands
his fingertips, becoming grapevines
left fruit all over her skin
this year the harvest
has never been richer

girl braids her hair into ropes
hangs them from her head and waits
for Prince Charming to come
rescue her from the tower that is girl

girl cannot wait
bites back tooth after tooth
until the dentist is screaming
feels the pronouns in her love poems
start to flicker like candles in a crypt
until her lips electrified
by cheap wine suddenly kiss –

girl is tired of being metaphor
wants to be simple human
is tired of being torn apart
in love letters
wants her breasts, eyes, and thighs
to remain together

with the rest of her
is tired of being asked
about her other half
as if she is not whole
girl is so, so tired

she remembers boy
wakes to the taste of him
every morning
remembers drinking
from the cups of his collarbones
she pushes him from her head
and back to the ocean
kisses the mirror instead
turns to her friend and says

I am enough
if mother to 10,000 children
or mother to none
we women carry a weight
about the neck
still our heads rise, and with a smile
we shoot darkness dead
and those who blew through my bed
like kisses from a train to the platform
do not make me

I am the ground
beneath the station
and the beat of that train leaving
is my pulse
I am a woman

and I am enough

YOU ARE NOT AN ALPHABET

nor is the earth a patchwork quilt
yet rust has started painting itself
into corners of your speech
there is a cattle grid
in every street

the sky is an empty duck egg
its pallor smiling weakly
like a mourner
over tea

you carefully note the birds
chaffinch, blue tit, thrush
submerge your watch
in the washing up
get your nails done
check the miniature shrine

watching lichen curl
pencil sharpenings
around a stiffening spine

THIS PATIENT SEA

1

he is losing himself
under a stack of medical papers
Grandma looks at him quietly
– thinks about the way you might
have to say a diagnosis out loud
three times before it is real

on holiday in Dartmouth
he gets lost drunk   she stays at home and I search from pub
        to pub
to see if they've had an elderly man
asking for red wine
by the bottle
he's found at 3am
mobility scooter mounting the kerb
wild hair haloing head
but the next day is frail
and we are scared again

the sea rubs shingle together
in its palm, knows this bit
on the shoreline   the wind
examines a ribcage
– the skeleton of a boat

2

the week before he died
I saw her cry for the first time
her newly hoarse voice shook
and I said something
like *oh, Grandma, I wish
I was there with you*
and she replied

with something
like *yes, well…*
I saw a lovely bird
in the garden yesterday
and wiped away her tears
before rattling on about nothing
like the last pill in the bottle

3

years later   it is her adrift
in prescriptions
the room is almost empty
apart from the stranger
that sits in her chair
sleeps in her bed, looks back
from the mirror
I doubt we will make it
to Dartmouth this year
the sea will have to wait

4

last night the Dart burst its banks
and travelled up the M5 to see her
there were no dams to stop it
trees and towns
were carefully avoided
not even a window pane got wet
the brackish water saw her
only as she had been
and soon she saw herself
as the same, but this morning
the saline came to us
in sealed bags

5

eight miles from Dartmouth
the pebble beach
of Slapton Sands sits
between the ocean and Slapton Ley
running the length of the bar
like a stitch is a single road

the stones here protect the coast
and cannot be replenished by the tide if taken
the sea curls in the bay
like an old dog asleep
at the end of the bed

THE GOLD AT OUR REACH

after Clara-Laeila Laudette

she walks the garden with scissors
dissecting this stem and that
the orange-handled blade's crunch
is crisp as a folded handkerchief
with creases ironed in

an accountant, with this
priceless haul of autumn, each petal
a fresh note, leaves falling from trees
    ruby acers
    forget-me-nots
    oak
all are pushed between paper
and months later released again
tissue-thin, translucent
ghost money
reaching us in other worlds
where committees of skyscrapers
look down
to see envelopes bearing our name
like a royal summons
handwritten thank-yous
birthday cards
bereavement notes

Sunday lunches at hers
in cold weather
with squirrels thieving nuts outside
and over milky tea
these things the city cannot give us
it tries too hard
with tin bowls, printed menus
but a smear of Colman's
on the side of the plate
– we know that this is true gold leaf

we know that the wealth is in the jar
and at a pressed flower card
arriving to greet a full table
with not one empty seat

UPON REALISING MY BODY IS A TEMPLE AND YOU WERE JUST HERE TO WORSHIP

you can cut glass
with a turn of your cheek
I read your actions like receipts
your gaze skips over my face
like a crack in the pavement
your arms are awkward
and by day
we are strangers

but at night
under the cover of sky
skin dyed by darkness
and cheekbones highlighted
by a streetlamp's gold

at night
you whisper words in my ear
that by daylight
illuminate my face from screens
at night the sheets sing
with the secrets of our skin
at night the air I breathe
tastes of your history
and I fall asleep to the sound
of the sea in your chest

with nights like these
I will accept any form of you
be it this
or the secondhand smoke
from the stranger
that speaks with your lips

I run, jump, freefall to land
on a seat on a train
as it skips beat by beat

tripping cross-country
I fall into my mother's arms
she feeds me words
laced with warnings
– this will end in tears
and they will not be his

see, loneliness isn't something
that happens when you're alone
it happens when you say
oh right
> *you don't mind*
> *if we sleep*
> *with other people as well*
it happens when I lie, say, *mind?*
I was thinking just the same thing myself

I feel it in the silence
when I've given you too much
let my month run away dreaming
of days filled with sunlit kisses
and your touch
or you claim me in crowded places
for everyone to see
please don't hide me in the dark
I'm tired of being Persephone

loneliness isn't something
that happens when you're alone
it's the realisation that that hand
that you're holding
is your own

but tonight
under the cover of this sky
I will hide this mess
and you'll whisper words in my ear
and I'll hear the sea in your chest

THE ONLY PLACE YOU CAN BE

I used to dream of being a spy
loved James Bond and to dress up
        to disguise
imagined hiding in tight places
erasing the boundary between me
and the rest
wanting what I didn't yet realise
was the charisma
of the promiscuous
and a really, really sharp suit

as I grew older
my dreams shifted, from Bond
to the bodies of his mistresses
and if the screen was a mirror
I couldn't see myself in it

dreams warped with waistlines
stretchmark seams
made me monster
half-woman, half-child, shapeshifting
sewn into this heavy, cumbersome
                wrong

but when the boys shouted
at least this body belonged to someone

so, hermit crabbing from one form
to the next, we used to joke
I was a B-cup for five minutes
and while curves tested the limits
of daily change
I used to dream of being cut back
like a wild garden, of pulling up
        the weeds of woman
that had sown seed under my ribs
and taken root

think that, maybe, with a little help
I could be beautiful too

it is not enough to simply tell someone they're wrong
when they tell you the space
they take up is a mistake
they need their silhouette shrunk

and to those who feel
like they don't belong
in the only place they can be

– my body, now not quite the same
shifting tides of womanhood settled on my frame
            sits still
now feels more me than my name
rests in the morning light of my eyes

I remember
what I would have given
for my fat to have torn
for my flesh to have worn down
to so much less
and I smile

see my skin, flesh, adorned
in only itself
isn't perfect
but my skin, flesh
adorned in only itself
is perfect

your body is beautiful and terrifying
            and it will take you so far
so batten down the hatches
tie your spine to the mast
this feeling you're feeling

it too shall pass

BUT I SPENT ALL EVENING INFLATING
THIS FOR YOU

yes, well, so did that clown
at the flower show
and they didn't try to put balloons
between my thighs and at least
they could make a small poodle
or something

my hair is full of splinters
and I hope that they stick
in your hand
that big fleshy garbage-pan lid
you call a hand
and that I have become a wasp
so you are poisoned by my bum
and that hand
it becomes bigger than you
than your dick
than your mother's first home

– didn't think of her, did you?
an enormous hand
a moon of hand
that crushes you
with a gravity

that erases your name
from my skin

but still you try to crowbar
my cheek

*does he not know
about my 10,000 teeth?*

*does he not know
what this jaw is for?*

LATE

eat   until there can't be room for anything else   be a complete
jigsaw and suffocate spaces   allow only tears   let them crawl
down skin like fingertips   watch the clock like a jealous lover
and remember   one in 3,197   one

be aware of a hand falling   to stomach trying to see through
skin   and muscle it is an animal   searching   catch it and tie
it up in the darkness of a pocket tighten fists

ask the asking to stop   if it is heard haunting the conversation
exorcise it with shopping lists politics   and prayer stop his lips
with the end of pens cigarettes and kisses

don't imagine   the doctor without wondering   how many
sleeping women have they put their hands inside   see
inquisitive digits   waiting to know inside better than anyone
at night dream of clean white   terrifying sheets and a cleaner
whiter   horrifying emptiness

wake   and make the effort to put this fear away to push it
between pages like a pressed flower   later make a beautiful
something of it   until then   keep hiding fragments across the
city   in corners under bridges

create anger at all that could change and direct it in a beam   a
needle pointed back pierce skin with bright cauterising heat
tomorrow say tomorrow   this will end

imagine blooming again   his relief will be like a homecoming
he'll hold in a sigh   like a steam train whistle and keep
fingers balled   inside his   as though   they have the
power to change this

now   feel a call   for something you cannot bring yourself to
understand across more   than an ocean

POSITIVE

thank god for your anxiety and love
for pissing on plastic sticks
as it was not so tough
for you 'caught it early'
like a prize fish

then it was just the small trick
the little snuff
a glass of water, a pill and a puff
of the cigarette I know
you were smoking
why did it happen after she moved?

I remember the time
you thought that Australia
was further from England
than the moon

now, with the miles arching
between our palms
it seems true

BRIGHTON PRIDE

for Martha

here they come and they are holding
each other's hands
like a stolen sceptre
like their fingers are lips
round the mouth of a snorkel
and that grasp, it's like gasping for air
or like they're holding some ticket
or a vital legal document
and they're on their way to the bank
or the airport and boarding a plane
for San Francisco, where they'll stay
for a week and ignore
all the landmarks
tell the Golden Gate Bridge
to go fuck itself
as their connected hands
are the only important construction
humanity has ever made

their fingers are the stitches
that bridge the river

their palms pressed above
– they are closing the wound

FIVE MINUTES BEFORE YOU ARRIVE

pull back your teeth
and take one deep breath
before like wood on the block
your lips split your face in two

I used to believe in stillness
and silence, but now my feet
are eggs in boiling water
when the heat of
your arrival comes
they threaten to crack
oh, what a stuttering
of kiss-interrupted words

sorry for my shaking hands
I borrowed them from my mother
each year she folds
the wrapping so carefully
and keeps this in darkness
for another year

in your absence, the world
has been thumbing her daily dead
through her fingers like a rosary
you have hung above me
like an hour of indecisions

welcome home

ACKNOWLEDGEMENTS

The Gold at Our Reach was originally written for a No Bindings event.

Thanks to Bridget Hart for such wonderful understanding and support throughout this. Thanks to Bridget and the Burning Eye team. Huge thanks to the fantastically special Bristol poetry scene. Big gloves to Liv Torc and the rest of the Hip Yak team.

Thanks to Charlie Williams for helping with the cover design.

Thanks to Ciaràn Hodgers, Patrick Downie and Georgia Elander for reading and listening to my poems with patience and solid advice.

Thanks to my mum for ensuring the words sing, and Dad for always hunting out all my terrible spelling.

And finally thank you to Dan, who's been there from the start.